Mia

by Iain Gray

Lang**Syne**

PUBLISHING

WRITING *to* REMEMBER

WRITING *to* REMEMBER

79 Main Street, Newtongrange,
Midlothian EH22 4NA
Tel: 0131 344 0414   Fax: 0845 075 6085
E-mail: info@lang-syne.co.uk
www.langsyneshop.co.uk

Design by Dorothy Meikle
Printed by Printwell Ltd
© Lang Syne Publishers Ltd 2016

ISBN 978-1-85217-531-3

Middleton

MOTTO:
Respect my right
(and)
Brave in difficulties.

CREST:
A hawk's head
(and)
A wolf's head
(and)
A lion rampant.

NAME variations include:
Midleton.

This is reflected in the famous *Domesday Book*, a massive survey of much of England and Wales, ordered by William I, to determine who owned what, what it was worth and therefore how much they were liable to pay in taxes to the voracious Royal Exchequer.

Completed in 1086 and now held in the National Archives in Kew, London, 'Domesday' was an Old English word meaning 'Day of Judgement.'

This was because, in the words of one contemporary chronicler, "its decisions, like those of the Last Judgement, are unalterable."

It had been a requirement of all those English landholders – from the richest to the poorest – that they identify themselves for the purposes of the survey and for future reference by means of a surname.

This is why the *Domesday Book*, although written in Latin as was the practice for several centuries with both civic and ecclesiastical records, is an invaluable source for the early appearance of a wide range of English surnames.

Several of these names were coined in connection with occupations.

These include Baker and Smith, while Cooks, Chamberlains, Constables and Porters were to be found carrying out duties in large medieval households.

The church's influence can be found in names such as Bishop, Friar and Monk while the popular name of Bennett derives from the late fifth to mid-sixth century Saint Benedict, founder of the Benedictine order of monks.

The early medical profession is represented by Barber, while businessmen produced names that include Merchant and Sellers.

Down at the village watermill, the names that cropped up included Millar/Miller, Walker and Fuller, while other self-explanatory trades included Cooper, Tailor, Mason and Wright.

Even the scenery was utilised as in Moor, Hill, Wood and Forrest – while the hunt and the chase supplied names that include Hunter, Falconer, Fowler and Fox.

Colours are also a source of popular surnames, as in Black, Brown, Gray/Grey, Green and White, and would have denoted the colour of the clothing the person habitually wore or, apart from the obvious exception of 'Green', one's hair colouring or even complexion.

The surname Red developed into Reid, while

Blue was rare and no-one wanted to be associated with yellow.

Rather self-important individuals took surnames that include Goodman and Wiseman, while physical attributes crept into surnames such as Small and Little.

Many families proudly boast the heraldic device known as a Coat of Arms, as featured on our front cover.

The central motif of the Coat of Arms would originally have been what was borne on the shield of a warrior to distinguish himself from others on the battlefield.

Not featured on the Coat of Arms, but highlighted on page three, is the family motto and related crest – with the latter frequently different from the central motif.

Adding further variety to the rich cultural heritage that is represented by surnames is the appearance in recent times in lists of the 100 most common names found in England of ones that include Khan, Patel and Singh – names that have proud roots in the vast sub-continent of India.

Echoes of a far distant past can still be found in our surnames and they can be borne with pride in commemoration of our forebears.

Chapter two:

Ancient roots

A locational surname that lends itself to a number of villages and towns of the name throughout England, 'Middleton' derives from the Middle English – via Old English – terms 'midel', indicating 'middle' and 'tun', indicating town.

Although particularly prevalent in Westmoreland from earliest times, the name is now found throughout the length and breadth of the British Isles.

In common with many other surnames that were popularised in the wake of the Norman Conquest of 1066, those who would come to bear it have roots that lie much further back in time.

This means that that flowing through the veins of many bearers of the name today may well be the blood of those Germanic tribes who invaded and settled in the south and east of the island of Britain from about the early fifth century.

Known as the Anglo-Saxons, they were composed of the Jutes, from the area of the Jutland Peninsula in modern Denmark, the Saxons from

Lower Saxony, in modern Germany and the Angles from the Angeln area of Germany.

It was the Angles who gave the name 'Engla land', or 'Aengla land' – better known as 'England.'

They held sway in what became England from approximately 550 to 1066, with the main kingdoms those of Sussex, Wessex, Northumbria, Mercia, Kent, East Anglia and Essex.

Whoever controlled the most powerful of these kingdoms was tacitly recognised as overall 'king' – one of the most noted being Alfred the Great, King of Wessex from 871 to 899.

It was during his reign that the famous *Anglo-Saxon Chronicle* was compiled – an invaluable source of Anglo-Saxon history – while Alfred was designated in early documents as *Rex Anglorum Saxonum*, King of the English Saxons.

Other important Anglo-Saxon works include the epic *Beowulf* and the seventh century *Caedmon's Hymn*.

Through the Anglo-Saxons, the language known as Old English developed, later transforming from the eleventh century into Middle English – sources from which many popular English surnames of today, such as Middleton, derive.

The Anglo-Saxons meanwhile, had usurped the power of the indigenous Britons – who referred to them as 'Saeson' or 'Saxones.'

It is from this that the Scottish Gaelic term for 'English people' of 'Sasannach' derives, the Irish Gaelic 'Sasanach' and the Welsh 'Saeson.'

Of Celtic pedigree, these early Britons were settled for centuries from a line south of the River Forth in Scotland all the way down to the south coast of England and with a particular presence in Wales.

Speaking a Celtic language known as Brythonic, they boasted a glorious culture that flourished even after the Roman invasion of Britain in 43 AD and the subsequent consolidation of Roman power by about 84 AD.

With many of the original Britons absorbing aspects of Roman culture, they became 'Romano-British' – while still retaining their own proud Celtic heritage.

We learn from the *Anglo-Saxon Chronicle* how the religion of the early Anglo-Saxons was one that pre-dated the establishment of Christianity in the British Isles.

Known as a form of Germanic paganism, with roots in Old Norse religion, it shared much in common with the Druidic 'nature-worshipping' religion of the indigenous Britons.

It was in the closing years of the sixth century that Christianity began to take a hold in Britain, while by approximately 690 it had become the 'established' religion of Anglo-Saxon England.

The first serious shock to Anglo-Saxon control came in 789 in the form of sinister black-sailed Viking ships that appeared over the horizon off the island monastery of Lindisfarne, in the northeast of the country.

The monastery was sacked in an orgy of violence and plunder, setting the scene for what would be many more terrifying raids on the coastline of not only England, but also those of Wales, Ireland and Scotland.

But the Vikings, or 'Northmen', in common with the Anglo-Saxons of earlier times, were raiders who eventually stayed – establishing, for example, what became Jorvik, or York, and the trading port of Dublin, in Ireland.

Through intermarriage, the bloodlines of the Anglo-Saxons also became infused with that of the Vikings.

But there would be another infusion of the

blood of the 'Northmen' in the wake of the Norman Conquest of 1066 – a key event in English history that sounded the death knell of Anglo-Saxon supremacy.

By this date, England had become a nation with several powerful competitors to the throne.

In what were extremely complex family, political and military machinations, the monarch was Harold II, who had succeeded to the throne following the death of Edward the Confessor.

But his right to the throne was contested by two powerful competitors – his brother-in-law King Harold Hardrada of Norway, in alliance with Tostig, Harold II's brother, and Duke William II of Normandy.

In what has become known as The Year of Three Battles, Hardrada invaded England and gained victory over the English king on September 20 at the battle of Fulford, in Yorkshire.

Five days later, however, Harold II decisively defeated his brother-in-law and brother at the battle of Stamford Bridge.

But he had little time to celebrate his victory, having to immediately march south from Yorkshire to encounter a mighty invasion force, led by Duke William of Normandy, that had landed at Hastings, in East Sussex.

Harold's battle-hardened but exhausted force of Anglo-Saxon soldiers confronted the Normans on October 14 in a battle subsequently depicted on the Bayeux tapestry – a 23ft. long strip of embroidered linen thought to have been commissioned eleven years after the event by the Norman Odo of Bayeux.

Harold drew up a strong defensive position at the top of Senlac Hill, building a shield wall to repel Duke William's cavalry and infantry.

The Normans suffered heavy losses, but through a combination of the deadly skill of their archers and the ferocious determination of their cavalry they eventually won the day.

Anglo-Saxon morale had collapsed on the battlefield as word spread through the ranks that Harold had been killed – the Bayeux Tapestry depicting this as having happened when the English king was struck by an arrow to the head.

Amidst the carnage of the battlefield, it was difficult to identify him – the last of the Anglo-Saxon kings.

Some sources assert William ordered his body to be thrown into the sea, while others state it was secretly buried at Waltham Abbey.

What is known with certainty, however, is

that William in celebration of his great victory founded Battle Abbey, near the site of the battle, ordering that the altar be sited on the spot where Harold was believed to have fallen.

William was declared King of England on December 25, and the complete subjugation of his Anglo-Saxon subjects followed.

Those Normans who had fought on his behalf were rewarded with the lands of Anglo-Saxons, many of whom sought exile abroad as mercenaries.

Within an astonishingly short space of time, Norman manners, customs and law were imposed on England – laying the basis for what subsequently became established 'English' custom and practice.

But beneath the surface, old Anglo-Saxon culture was not totally eradicated, with some aspects absorbed into those of the Normans, while faint echoes of the Anglo-Saxon past is still seen today in the form of popular surnames such as Middleton.

It is a name that features prominently in the frequently turbulent historical record.

During the bitter seventeenth century English Civil War, John Middleton, 1st Earl of Middleton, born in about 1608 into a family that had held lands in Scotland from as early as the twelfth century, was the soldier who, in common with many others, found himself conflicted in his loyalties.

The war had been sparked off when the Catholic monarch Charles I had incurred the wrath of Parliament by his insistence on the 'divine right' of kings.

Added to this was Parliament's fear of Catholic 'subversion' against the state and the king's stubborn refusal to grant demands for religious and constitutional concessions.

Matters came to a head with the outbreak of the war in 1642, with Parliamentary forces, known as the New Model Army and commanded by Oliver Cromwell and Sir Thomas Fairfax, arrayed against the Royalist army of the king.

In what became an increasingly bloody and complex conflict, spreading to Scotland and Ireland and with rapidly shifting loyalties on both sides, the king was eventually captured and executed in January of 1649 on the orders of Parliament.

John Middleton had for a time fought for the cause of the ill-fated Charles I, before switching allegiance in favour of his son Charles II, while as an opponent of Charles I, he played a role in one of his major military defeats in Scotland.

A bitter civil war had raged in Scotland between the forces of those Presbyterian Scots who had signed a National Covenant that opposed the divine right of the Stuart monarchy and Royalists such as James Graham, 1st Marquis of Montrose, whose prime allegiance was to Charles I.

Although Montrose had initially supported the Covenant, his conscience later forced him to switch sides – resulting in his great campaigns from 1644 to 1645, that became known as the Year of Miracles because of his brilliant military successes.

At the battle of Inverlochy, on February 2, 1645, the Covenanter the Earl of Argyll was forced to ignominiously flee in his galley after 1,500 of his force was wiped out in a surprise attack.

What makes Montrose's victory all the more notable is that his hardy forces had arrived at Inverlochy after an exhausting 36-hour march south through knee-deep snow from the area of the present-day Fort Augustus.

Montrose had a great victory at Kilsyth on August 15, 1645, but final defeat came at Philiphaugh, near Selkirk, less than a month later – with John Middleton playing a key role in command of some of the parliamentary troops that defeated him.

Created Earl of Middleton by Charles II following his Restoration in 1660, he was appointed Lord High Commissioner to the Parliament of Scotland – later serving before his death in 1674 as governor of Tangier, on the coast of Morocco.

In a much later century, and also on the bloody field of battle, Rawdon Hume Middleton, better known as Ron Middleton, was an Australian recipient of the Victoria Cross (VC), the highest award for valour in the face of enemy action for British and Commonwealth forces.

Born in 1916 in Waverley, Sidney, he enlisted in the Royal Australian Air Force in 1940, joining No.149 Squadron of the Royal Air Force (RAF) in February of 1942 as a bomber pilot.

In November of that year, piloting a Stirling BF 372 returning from a raid over an aircraft factory in Italy, his bomber was heavily damaged by anti-aircraft fire.

Through his piloting skills and despite being badly wounded and drifting in and out of consciousness, he managed to retain control of his aircraft long enough for seven of his crew to safely bail out.

Middleton was killed when the stricken

bomber eventually ditched in the English Channel.

Honoured in 1995 on an Australian postage stamp, his VC is now on display at the Australian War Memorial, Canberra.

Chapter three:

Honours and distinction

Bearers of the proud name of Middleton have achieved fame through a wide range of pursuits and endeavours.

Born in 1726 in Leith, the son of a customs collector, Admiral Charles Middleton was the naval officer and politician who played a key role in British naval affairs during the 1756 to 1763 Seven Years War with France and the 1775 to 1783 American War of Independence.

Enlisting in the Royal Navy when he was aged 16, he later served as a lieutenant during the Seven Years War and was responsible, aboard HMS *Anson*, for the capture of two French ships.

Of a volatile temperament, he was court-martialed in 1757 after physically attacking a sailor over an argument involving rum rations but was returned to favour two years later when he was given command of the frigate HMS *Arundel*.

In 1758 he was responsible for the capture of no fewer than sixteen French ships.

During the American War of Independence,

he acted in the important role of Comptroller of the Navy, while in 1781 he was raised to the Peerage of the United Kingdom as 1st Baronet Barham, of Barham Court and Teston in the County of Kent.

Elected Tory Member of Parliament (MP) three years later for Rochester, he became a leading advocate for the abolition of the slave trade in the British Empire – having been influenced by many examples of its inhuman practice that he had witnessed during his time on the high seas.

The slave trade was eventually abolished six years before his death in 1813, while he is recognised as having played an important political role in this landmark British Parliamentary ruling.

On American shores, Arthur Middleton is recognised as one of the Founding Fathers of the United States as a signatory on July 4, 1776 of the American Declaration of Independence.

Born in 1742 in Charleston, South Carolina to parents who had emigrated from England, he studied law before entering politics during the American War of Independence.

It was as a member of what was known as the Continental Congress, representing Carolina, that he signed the Declaration of Independence, while during the War of Independence, also known as the American Revolutionary War, he served in the American ranks during the defence of Charleston.

Described by his contemporaries as a 'steady unshaken patriot, gentleman and scholar', he died in 1787.

In much more contemporary times, Catherine Elizabeth Middleton, born in 1982 and growing up in the small village of Chapel Row, near Newbury in Berkshire, is better known as Kate Middleton and by her official royal title of Catherine, Duchess of Cambridge.

It was while studying the history of art at St Andrews University, Scotland, that in 2001 she met fellow student Prince William, then Prince William of Wales.

Now Prince William, Duke of Cambridge, he is second in line to the British throne.

The couple's engagement was announced in November of 2010, while they married in April of the following year in an internationally publicised ceremony in Westminster Abbey.

They are now the proud parents of George, Prince of Cambridge, born in 2013, and Charlotte, Princess of Cambridge, born in 2015.

Not of aristocratic roots herself, Kate's parents worked for British Airways before founding their own highly successful mail order company that sells party supplies and decorations.

Their other daughter, Philippa Charlotte Middleton, better known as Pippa Middleton, born in 1983, is the English socialite who, in common with her older sister, is a favourite of media photographers.

Chapter four:

On the world stage

Born in Vancouver, British Columbia in 1922, the daughter of an actress, Marie De Carlo, and a salesman, William Middleton, Margaret Yvonne Middleton was the actress better known by her stage name of Yvonne De Carlo.

Taken as a teenager by her mother to Hollywood to enrol in a dancing school, she went on to become a major star of both the big screen and television.

Her film credits include the 1942 *This Gun for Hire*, the 1943 *For Whom the Bell Tolls*, the 1947 *Song of Scheherazade*, the 1956 *The Ten Commandments* – in the role of Sephira – and, from 1991, *Oscar*.

She is best known, however, for her role of Lily Munster in the popular television series of 1964 to 1966, *The Munsters*, while other television credits include *Bonanza*, the 1977 mini-series *Roots* and *Murder, She Wrote*.

The recipient of a star on the Hollywood Walk of Fame, she died in 2007.

Born in 1874 in Elizabeth Town, Kentucky, **Charles B. Middleton** was the American actor of stage and film best known for his role of Ming the Merciless in the *Flash Gordon* series of films, and as a descendant of the United States Declaration of Independence signatory Arthur Middleton – referred to in the previous chapter.

It was after working in travelling circuses and vaudeville that he entered the film industry.

In addition to starring as Ming the Merciless in the three *Flash Gordon* films from 1936 to 1940 – *Flash Gordon*, *Flash Gordon's Trip to Mars* and *Flash Gordon Conquers the Universe* – he also had other film credits that include the 1931 *Safe in Hell*, the 1932 *The Strange Love of Molly Brown* and the 1940 *Abe Lincoln in Illinois*.

Married to the American stage and film actress Leora Spellman, he died in 1949.

Behind the radio microphone, **Cecil Henry Middleton**, better known to his listeners as "Mr Middleton", was the gardener and writer who was one of the first gardening radio broadcasters for the BBC.

Born in 1886 in Northamptonshire, he became famous during the Second World War for his weekly *Dig for Victory* broadcasts that encouraged the war-torn British public to cultivate their own plots in whatever gardening space was available to them.

He also hosted the *Kitchen Front* programme – which is also recognised as having had a major effect on wartime food production by the public.

It is estimated, for example, that in the particularly dark days of the war in 1942 more than 70% of the British population regularly tuned in to his broadcasts.

But, despite his vital contribution to the war effort, when his home in London was bombed out during the blitz and he had to temporarily relocate to live with relatives outwith London, the BBC bureaucracy dismissed his claim for a travelling allowance as "grabbing."

In later years, however, an official BBC history noted of him that: "In four years, he guided a new national movement towards self-sufficiency. It would be hard to write a social history of the war years without mentioning Mr Middleton."

Also a popular columnist for the *Daily Express* newspaper and recognised as Britain's first 'celebrity' gardener, he died in September of 1945 – only a few weeks after the official end of the Second World War.

In the creative world of the written word, **Stanley Middleton** was the British novelist born in 1919 in Bulwell, Nottinghamshire.

A teacher of English for many years, his acclaimed works include *Holiday*, winner in 1974 of the prestigious Booker Prize, the 1960 *Harris's Requiem*, the 1968 *The Golden Virtue* and the 1971 *Brazen*.

For reasons that remain unclear, before his death in 2009 he declined the offer of an MBE in recognition of his distinguished literary output.

Born in Christchurch, New Zealand in 1925, Osmand Edward Middleton, better known as **O.E. Middleton**, was the short-story writer whose internationally best-selling works include his 1959 *The Stone and Other Stories* and the 1998 *The Big Room and Other Stories*.

The recipient of a New Zealand Book Award for his anthology *Selected Stories*, he died in 2010.

He was the older brother of the novelist **Ian Middleton**, born in 1928 and whose work before his death in 2007 includes the 1979 *Pet Shop*, the 1995 *Harvest* and, from 1997, *I See a Voice*.

Born in 1880 in Paterson, New Jersey, **George Middleton** was the American playwright, director and producer who, while serving from 1927 to 1929 as president of the Dramatists' Guild of America, created what is known as the Minimum Basic Agreement for determining theatrical royalties.

Author of works that include his 1947 *These Things are Mine*, he died in 1967.

In the sciences, **Gerard Middleton**, born in South Africa in 1931 and who settled in Canada when aged 23, is the leading geologist who specialises in the fields of not only sedimentology and geological data analysis but also in the history of the subject.

A professor in the school of geography and earth sciences at McMaster University in Hamilton, Ontario, he is the author of a number of pioneering works on geology that include his 1972 *Origin of Sedimentary Rocks*, while he is also a Fellow of the Royal Society of Canada.

In the world of contemporary music, **Malcolm Middleton**, born in Dumfries in 1973, is the Scottish musician best known for his work with the band Arab Strap – and whose own highly successful 2002 solo album is the decidedly oddly named *5:14 Fluoxytin Seagull Alcohol John Nicotine*.

On a particularly infamous and gruesome note, **David Middleton** is the only convicted American serial killer to date to have served in the trusted position of a police officer.

Born in 1961, it was after having served as an officer with the Miami police force that, in August of 1994, he murdered by suffocation in Sun Valley, Nevada, 45-year-old Thelma Davila.

While the hunt for her killer spread throughout the United States, in February of the following year he murdered the schoolteacher Katherine Powell – again by strangulation by a cable and giving rise to his macabre media nickname of "The Cable Guy."

Eventually tracked down, he was arrested and brought to trial and sentenced to death in September of 1997.

Still waiting on Death Row to pay the ultimate price for his heinous crimes, he is also suspected of having committed other murders.

Returning to the original derivation of the Middleton name from a number of villages and towns throughout the length and breadth of the British Isles, one indication of its ancient roots is the present-day 'new city' of Milton Keynes, in the English county of Buckinghamshire, and which is built around what was the humble hamlet known as Middletone.

Developed during the late 1960s, Milton Keynes still proudly retains what is known as Milton Keynes Village which, in turn, was the village of Middletone and later 'Middleton de Keynes.'

Raising a glass in honour of proud bearers of the Middleton name – in the form of the spelling variation 'Midleton' – *Midleton Very Rare* is an Irish premium blended whisky that has been produced by Irish Distillers from the East Cork town of Midleton since 1984.

One of the finalists in the 2011 *Ultimate Spirits Challenge Awards* and earning the accolade of "Extraordinary – Ultimate Recommendation", it is produced in only strictly limited quantities, with only fifty of the casks of the golden nectar being released every year.